The Unpainted Shore

Cover design by Jen Lambert
Cover Art courtesy of Noah Jackson

Book design by Liz Kay

ISBN: 978-0-9897837-1-2

Published by Spark Wheel Press

The Unpainted Shore

C Dylan Bassett

Spark Wheel Press

Omaha, NE

For Ked and Erin

Contents

The unpainted shore, accepts the world,
As anything but sculpture.

—Wallace Stevens

October

It was October after my father died. All the fountains sealed. I walked through the garden unapologetically. Correction: I was the garden and it was painful to be a body. Dark birds covered me. Correction: I was a murder of dark birds moving from roof to roof. Correction: I was a murmur. I drank the rain.

It was October, my mind. A flashlight clicking inside the storm. Confession: I didn't wake and I couldn't help it. Outside: the sound of ice, and the night turned over to ask: What do white walls say? How could I answer.

I rearranged the old rooms: the chair facing the wall, the window facing the chair, the world facing the window. The tedium of a mantel clock's summon. Loosely a fly banged against a lightbulb.

Of the sun, its blaze: it did not seek me. I heard the bleat of geese migrating through the firmament. The traffic's drone as if I were sleeping. I touched the mud and I was made of it. Twigs, or flecks of skin. A vessel void of organs. A name without an image. My hand covered my mouth exactly.

I wandered October according to the laws. A less-than-certain wind, a stranger's touch. My father's body, a cicatrix of autumn leaves. Mechanical theology, broken radio reception, voices of the dead. Each word, another trespass. He was always there until I looked. He was always there. My father's body, a candle flame quivering.

Lake Effect

When they find him his pockets are full of water. (He was always in the background like a candle.)

People want to know why it happened, what's on the other side of a wall. Like any narrative, this one has something to find.

Some lakes are so deep they can swallow an entire human. Policemen photograph the empty shore.

The spoons have clattered. The curtains have been drawn to enclose the unmade bed. A figure in the pillow humming.

Erosion is a painting, meaning without speech. I am erasing what I can.

(I do not recall what I said, or whether I spoke aloud at all.)

The house is the room is the body is gone. The water rushing through me is incurable. It seems strange to say we would not know each other now.

The shelves are empty is everyone's lifetime. No trace continues, a period of gray.

It is always with another's key that I unlock the house.

These people remind me of real people.

If there is a protagonist in this story, then one way of seeing him is here, waiting in the empty bath.

The day is an astronomical distance like those before it. A proliferation, an account and recounting. A mouse crawls in and out of my shadow in search of a crumb.

I said I wanted to live. (I don't know why I said that.)

A figure confined to a room takes on the spirit of the room. In sleep and in dormancy he comes very close to death. His face hardens as in a picture.

The house darkens before I notice it. Moonlight, a rope that can't be climbed, lines the contours of objects—the table, the kitchen knives. A moth gets caught in the keyhole.

The desires to build and break are equal, a habit of thought, a wedge of light beneath a door in an otherwise unlit closet.

My insomnia, my involuntary vigil—the grainy birds are also awake, like me except the reverse, tossing themselves against the brick—consumes me.

Everyone is alone but exactly how no one can say.

The wife, the baby, the backyard. It's all in his head. (He speaks as if still early in the morning.)

We've killed each other in previous dreams.

(A small hotel in the middle of the day, a cable that once restrained a dog.)

The rain turns to snow, spilling across the windshield like sideway tears.

The field's expanse bends the curvature of earth, a tree is pure mindlessness.

He wanted to talk about the future. A horse ran in circles.

In another version: the lake is full of ruined bikes. A hand which is a hammer which is a fist. A constant voice on either side of me, or a mask waiting to be worn.

The lake is nothing's parable. You have to move very fast in order to stay in place.

Selfhood occurs, but merely as proxy. My face is a mirror, other faces come and go.

The gate swings a draft. The hallway is always changing shape with me inside it, a perpetual latitude.

I note the routine sunrise, how long have I been awake?

The whisper of a spinning ring: a body enters the water, ripples move away from land.

Trash drifts across the yard as in a film. The actual day of death is arbitrary. God, or medicine. A story on the news.

Imagine a world where everyone plays with dolls. A deer drowns in a swimming pool and nobody cries.

A theory of the lake is dark spot on the landscape. A book whose pages are blank. A depth of unknown limit. A mouth nearly blue.

In my line of vision, the faint contour of a cloud and child. A branch reaches across the window as if disembodied.

What the mind fails to contain. I wear someone else's clothing.

The distance between the day and the night is two birds.

The eyes are little hands, they work by being open. To blink is akin to drawing a portrait, and in this case, a portrait of my father sleeping.

I find a wing frozen on the windshield of my car and do not remove it.

A certain declination occurring at midday, the slow noise of a mouth beginning to close.

The tide is an interruption, as in the barrel of a gun. It hurts the eye.

The tide is retrospective. What was lost or gained in weeks of my indecision.

Like any narrative, this one contains a church, or the possibility of a church. Talking about myself, I use the pronoun "he." As in "then he was alone" or "he could use more sunlight."

How many lakes will fit inside one body?

He looks the same in every picture, I said. And why not, I said. At some point in the future, the past will include music that never really existed.

Everyone chooses to hear certain words. I hear "name," and later "no."

This is how we never arrive. This is a lion. This is a coffin with a snowflake. This is the lake where his body used to move.

This is me: idle and spinning my canoe.

I look into the dim water mirror of stars. I reach out to touch them but touch my own face.

Steam rises from a cup of tea like penance. An apple begins to fall.

Is the flock one thing or many? And the crowd of black umbrellas? And the weather?

(See the hat with no head. The panicked rabbit strangled in wire.)

Oh the ambiguity (someone said).

Sleep has no conclusion. I still feel close to him. (Not close enough to touch.)

The water lapping against the hull invokes a horror in its periodicity. Its repetition, a constant border in which I am rendered immobile. Useless.

My mind enters a blank state called "religious." Who can remember which day it is?

I cross the bridge and it feels correct. God is a girl inside of a boy inside of a baby. A map drawn in haste.

The dogs bark at something that never arrives, form no longer lording over matter. A ghost can be anything, a stray glove.

I heard clothes rustling on the stairs (though it could have been something else).

Someone's yelling out there. A more permanent snowstorm. That's me at the corner table pretending to be an adult, pretending to wait for someone.

"You're leaving so soon?" "But what about the fog?"

I look through a window and a window looks back. (Looks nothing like God.)

To see is a grain of salt. One must learn it. Learn it again. The eyes adjust in the dark but not yet. The space does not exist until I step into it.

The lake does not exist until he steps into it.

A painted sky shadows the sun. The flags are gone but not the wind. There aren't that many people on earth.

Enclosures

The body is less a fire more a fire pit.

A winter beyond the jurisdiction

of lamplight. Elsewhere, the rush of animals

waking. A crow becomes something entirely else,

in this case, time like a network of jolting wings.

The body is not dead but dormant, a firetruck

at the bottom of a lake. Winter is

a waiting game. Snow repeats

snow repeats snow.

It wakes to the heater's warble,

the refrigerator clicking off, the sound

of a book closing, or a radio tuned inexactly,

the wind overtaking the trees. It hears

the clatter of ice in a glass of water,

reminding the body

of its father, who wandered

into a lake and never came back.

The body paces, reciting the names

of its shoes. It encounters the doorknob

like a foreign language. It moves inside a shell

the exact shape of itself. It thinks its hands

have swollen but cannot be sure. Again,

the body thinks it. Water rises all around

but there is no water. The planets watch

with the porcelain eyes of dolls.

The body emerges from the shower.

It looks in the mirror and its dead father

looks back. "No," I say, "that's my chin,

my sunken cheekbones."

Winter takes everything

as usual, an opera of extravagant pauses.

Stillness expanding like an intruder entering

the room. It lies at the foot of the stairs,

fluent in hook and spoon. Strange, it

thinks, how a single boat defines the horizon.

How a river vanishes into an eye.

In a storm, the body tends to the window

like a dog left at home. It cannot be sure

whether what it feels is love or hunger.

The body remembers the childhood piano.

The faucet lightly running.

The telephone ringing all afternoon

behind a locked door.

The body is unrecognizable more

recently. Hair grows away from the skin

as if wanting to escape.

Quietly the body is given

to oblivion: a fly in a spoonful of sugar,

a rattling in the ring box, an unraveling

of fine wire. The ongoing fear of thunder

and thunder and inadequate hands.

The body holds the moon

reflected in a broken cup.

How it forgets to lock the front door. How

it throws the jacket over the banister. How it sleeps

in its shoes. How it dreams of oars tearing

the sea apart. How it wakes unsure whether

it's morning or night. How an eyelash

hits the floor. How it searches

for a pulse, then finds one.

I resent what I am now: lacking

the capacity for faith, existing

the way paint exists on a wall. I am defined

by my breath, or by my facial features,

my ability to speak without opening

my mouth, without transition.

The room fills with shadows,

none of them human.

The body looks in the mirror and sees

another mirror. Itself watching itself watching.

The coffee gets cold, a sheet of milk

spreading across. Death prevents the dead

from being understood but not

from speaking. What does it mean,

the bird flying in circles around

the lighthouse. The churches

and the empty chair.

Death shakes the body into

something other than itself. An echo. A blade

of grass. What the body has is what

the body lost. A voice inside a dream.

Through a window, it sees

the lakeshore, the waves chasing each other

down. Snow falls loudly on the small house.

Above the snow, the sky.

Elegy

(Everyone talking at once but in another room. They never mention him by his full name. Everyone has an idea, what he did or why, which medication he took. I leave the television on for the noise. It doesn't matter, someone says. Tomorrow is yesterday already. Most people have been dead a long time, someone says. Why bring it up again? The bed anticipates the body's absence, empty as in the page. It's easy to write the word.)

it's like the desire to be a soldier
to lose a war on purpose

home is impossible, you said
we cannot hear the hummingbirds

(I talk to him on the phone for an hour then remember he's dead. A butterfly beats unevenly behind a curtain, the body fighting back. Does solitude make one more beautiful or less? In my dream he's walking away again. Soon he reaches the water. Things will get darker before they get totally black. His jacket is black, his hair.)

I wake to the ignition jump of a car
leaving, left

a fly breaks my eye's momentum
lures my vision along a string

the blue is empty except for its sky
a lake that mirrors

the geese diving
without knowing the difference

once, alone, you
insisted you saw

a deer stepping out of its skin

(A camera sees the subject unmoved. The subject is seen through a lens. A description of the subject's wet shirt. The description of time allegedly. The police officer gestures a sinking ship. The description of hands, an indication of struggle. The description of weather. The notable absence of green. A stranger in the crowd who never speaks. I do not speak. The siren obscures the background. The vague supplication. The face unabridged. A fact. The subject is lit by camera flash.)

what I try to forget the snow
remembers

a real snow that doesn't fall

an entire family
abandoning their home
the blankets still folded

death moves
but only one way

I paint the roof to look
like snow

(Why don't you just tell me the words and I'll say them.)

the body is gone but the breath remains

a horse in a meadow
falls before it's shot

a horse who is dead has the eyes
of a man

it makes a sound
not even God understands

a tongue inside a stone

(Memories occur in flashes but more frequently. A threshold condition. An image that builds matter around itself, like time in the past. I wake up and wait for what. I calculate the aluminum sky in photographs, tracing its framework. Tracing it over again. Death was a smaller story when I was young, a bed was called a bed and looked like one. On the radio they say winter is crossing the mountains. Sirens in looms of cloud. Whomever I dream is alive.)

briefly I catch myself reflected
but no one's here to witness it

aspirin unravels in a glass of water

where a boat begins to sink
the world is

a rumor I tell myself

a prayer ends without thunder

a dog runs
from a paper fire

(In another dream, we call each other by different names. We wear our hands on the wrong wrists. No ambulance yet, no telephones ringing. Provoked by revision, I do not take my eyes off him, do not blink. The sky is so bright I cannot see the sky, the grass is green and perfectly cut.)

there's so few days and thousands
of miles, almost

nobody is ready
I know the way home, or

I'm just driving

a lake rises
taller than itself
taller

than the figure who stands
inside it

the tide churning
like insomnia

("I always believed I was watching a movie instead of living a life. Sometimes there was a blizzard. I was trying to escape is one explanation.")

a bathtub overflows into the dream
words fall out of a sentence

was it an accident?
was it real?

on the day you die, a woman
spills wine on her white dress

a gunshot scatters
the deer like blood

(At first you only see his fingers. Later: the coarse hair, the discolored torso. A fog kicks up into which an airplane descends. How much will the body change before it isn't his?)

when will I become invisible, you said
and I said, people see

each other everywhere
I saw a face

in the bottom of a bowl
and I tapped it with a spoon

(The burred edge of things. Wind arrives from no direction, apples in the yard rot. They stain the dirt they lie in. My collar is damp beneath my neck. My toes tear my socks. The body moves in habit. In another version, I turn wind back into a word. I am toys bobbing in a swimming pool.)

the cup breaks because I can't
hold onto it

how do you define
dreams: everything

is the same except lost

tightly the earth
turns away

I am building

a ghost out of a body

(As if to erase my eyelids. Extended contact with the mirror. It's midnight and I'm still breathing. What the mirror complicates, a distance within proximity. A stranger wears black in another room. The dread of seeing or being seen. I have heard a ghost loves nothing new and so I sleep in the same sheets. Whatever trees do, I do the opposite. The days of and so on. Now is just beginning. And now.)

Acknowledgements

I'd like to thank the editors of the following journals where some of these poems first appeared, often in different forms: *Bodega, Caketrain, the Cincinnati Review, CutBank, Copper Nickel, Dear Sir, Hayden's Ferry Review, Jellyfish, the Laurel Review, Memorious, the Pinch, Pleiades, Prairie Schooner* and *Subtropics.*

Lake Effect was originally published as a chapbook by Thrush Press, thank you Helen Vitoria and Ocean Vuong.

Thank you to Liz Kay, Jen Lambert and everyone at Spark Wheel Press for caring about this book and bringing it into print.

Thank you to Dan Beachy-Quick, Anthony Cinquepalmi, Carolina Ebeid, Summer Ellison, Matthew Fee, James Galvin, Winter Goebel, Susan Elizabeth Howe, Will Jameson, Kimberly Johnson, Richard Kenny, Lance Larsen, Hannah Loeb, Jamaal May, Cassidy McFadzean, Fatima Mirza, Jack Murphy, Elyse Mele, Petro Moysaenko, D.A. Powell, Parker Smith, Joe Sherlock, Bryce Thronburg, Jean Valentine, Joseph Verica, G.C. Waldrep and Emma Winsor Wood for their encouragement, support and insight.

I am especially grateful to Kylan Rice without whom I would be lost.

About the Author

C Dylan Bassett is the author of *The Invention of Monsters / Plays for the Theatre* (Plays Inverse Press 2015) and five additional chapbooks. His poems have appeared in journals such as *Black Warrior Review*, *Columbia*, *Diagram*, and *Salt Hill*. He is teaching fellow at the Iowa Writers' Workshop.

www.ingramcontent.com/pod-product-compliance
Lightning Source LLC
Chambersburg PA
CBHW081538040426
42447CB00014B/3412